Murilo Vinicius Teles
Diego Antonio

Development of a web platform for bands and musicians

Murilo Vinicius Teles
Diego Antonio

Development of a web platform for bands and musicians

Plataforma DivulgaSom Promote your sound!

ScienciaScripts

Cover image: www.ingimage.com

This book is a translation from the original published under ISBN 978-613-9-72217-4.

Publisher:
Sciencia Scripts
is a trademark of
Dodo Books Indian Ocean Ltd. and OmniScriptum S.R.L publishing group

120 High Road, East Finchley, London, N2 9ED, United Kingdom
Str. Armeneasca 28/1, office 1, Chisinau MD-2012, Republic of Moldova, Europe
Printed at: see last page
ISBN: 978-620-7-94179-7

ACKNOWLEDGEMENTS

We couldn't fail to mention the names of the people who have been so present throughout our academic life and especially in the preparation of this work:

To the Paula Souza Centre for the opportunity;

To the Faculty of Technology of Tatuí, for the academic training;

To professors Pedro Santa Rosa, Samuel Antonio, Clovis de Souza, Carlos Alberto, Walter Masson, Eoná Moro, Patrícia Glaucia, Paula Hypolito, Ferreira, Antônio Carlos, Marcos Lopes, Élide, Katia, Mauricio, Geraldo, Ovídio, José Carlos Ferreira, Paulo Rubens, Cesar Sacco, Cesario de Moraes, José Mathias, Osvaldo Rosica, Rosana and many others for their wisdom and patience in shaping our ideas; To our parents and family, for their support, affection and presence whenever necessary;

My dear Taverna, who gave me all the support I needed and more.

To our special friends: Roberto Carriel, Nilton Jeongyeon, Drezim Ferrarezi, Luiz Oliveira IV, Super To, Paulo DBZ, Wilian Casa, Naniel Tomé, FelipeKratosNarutoYubel, Vitoria Nogueira, Carolina de Nicola, Juliana Soares, Teuz Roza, Mumu Souza, Daniel GTA, Jhonny, Jojo Sana, Felipe Furue, Tainan Camargo, Ailton Leme, Stefani Alves, Maiza Dias, Elliene Florenscia, Otavio Henrique, João Guilherme, Nathalia Campos, Karina Camargo, Gabriel Maciel,Aparicio, Jeff de Paula, Gusinho Henrique, Thauani Ortolani, Rodrigo Delazari, Nicoly Crescencio, Vinimon Moraes, Isamon Porto, Denis Nogueira, Lucas Shoque, João Bazooka, Mauricio Filho, Mauricio MauMau, Wanderlei VanVan, Thiago Macena, Felipe Rosa, Amanda Bumaruf, Deivide Paulino, Giovanna Brusetti, Giovana Modena and everyone else for their help, inspiration and the affection of fellow students and friends.

...I haven't seen golden dreams yet (Robert "Jetboy" Tomlin)

When everything seems to be going wrong in your life, remember that the plane takes off against the wind, not in its favour

(Henry Ford).

SUMMARY

Music has always been present in human life. Since its inception, it has been associated with the state of mind of human beings as a way of expressing their feelings. With the development of professional activities, music began to be worked in the commercial sector and since then there have been many challenges for professionals in the field. As a result, some areas of work, such as the music of individual professionals and amateur bands, have not been properly publicised. However, the advance of technology has led to growth in different sectors, especially in terms of publicising personal and professional work. Everywhere there are undiscovered musicians and bands with potential who are not recognised. In Tatuí, known as the capital of music, the city in which this project is being developed, there are a large number of musicians and bands with great musical knowledge and potential, but who are unable to make a living from their musical work due to a lack of better publicity. This also happens in neighbouring towns. In this context, the general aim of this undergraduate project was to use information technology and digital marketing to develop career prospects for amateur musicians and bands, by creating a web platform for publicising, hiring online and improving communication between client and applicant. The specific objectives were: to describe the shortcomings in the promotion of musicians and amateur bands; to identify the requirements and tools used to solve the problem; to develop a web platform for promotion; and to test and analyse the promotion of musicians and amateur bands. Digital marketing techniques were used to promote musicians and bands. The following materials and methods were used to develop the site: computer, smartphone, books, programming language and surveys of musicians and bands. The language used for development was HTML, the standard language for web pages, as well as PHP for communication with the MySql database, in which all the musicians' data was stored, and JavaScript, for greater interaction between the site and users. The mechanism for adding style to a CSS web document was also applied, which is responsible for the layout design and responsiveness of the site so that it can be adapted to all desktop and mobile platforms. The development environment was Notepad++ and WampServer. This tool must meet the communication needs of the client and the service, since the site is only for communication and will not fulfil any kind of financial contract. It is hoped that with this platform individual musicians and amateur bands will be able to publicise their work and gain space and relevance in the music market.

Keywords: Musicians and Bands, Digital Marketing, Web Platform Development.

SUMMARY

CHAPTER 1

INTRODUCTION

Nowadays, with the advance of information technology, the world has gone digital and some professions that used to be advertised mostly in personal dialogues, posters or radio and television commercials, have now lost the opportunity to be publicised in society. One case in point is musicians and amateur bands, who in many places are not properly publicised.

It's very common for most actions to work through technology and social networks, but some actions are still not fully utilised through it, such as publicising bands and amateur singers. Usually, publicity and hiring are done informally or even through relatives, referrals and people close to them. There are unknown bands with considerable potential, but with few resources and recognition. This causes them to give up their careers and look for other professions.

In this context, with the combination of the internet and digital marketing, which uses tools for targeted and agile dissemination of work virtually, there will be a significant improvement in the promotion of musicians and bands, especially in the city of Tatuí and the region where this work is being developed and applied.

Digital marketing brings great benefits to the commercial area. According to Loprete and Loprete (2009), digital marketing is a way of marketing using the tools available on the Internet, such as websites, banners, e-mails and so on. This type of marketing has numerous advantages such as comfort, speed, lower costs, information, closer relationships and the possibility of receiving more detailed data.

Looking at the advantages of digital marketing applied in various areas, but specifically in the area of music, it is possible to better publicise musicians and amateur bands. Therefore, the purpose of this graduation project is to develop a website, based on a detailed study of the requirements of this need, with the aim of boosting the promotion of musicians and amateur bands. With this tool, it's possible to make the music industry stand out in the market and give amateurs a better chance of success by making them more recognised and also helping them financially with their performances.

1.1 JUSTIFICATION

There are common needs among music bands. One of these needs, and the one that stands out the most, is the difficulty musicians have in finding a way to properly publicise their work when they leave their musical training course, becoming victims of informality. This informality exists in all types of service. In the case of our graduation work, informality is present in the issue of hiring musicians, which is done through conventional and unconventional means such as referrals from acquaintances, word of mouth and, for the most part, through social networks such as Facebook, Instagram and even Youtube, which most musicians, even professionals, use to publicise their work.

Such a platform would be able to provide a kind of link between these informalities, making it easier for the contractor to access the musician and making hiring less informal. In addition, there is a great need for a specialised advertising tool in the music sector, since such specialisation would make it easier for the contractor to find a specific platform that provides as much information about the musician as possible. Another factor that influenced the origin of this graduation project is the diversity of music in the world. There are currently hundreds of different musical styles and, in some cases, musicians of certain styles may not receive due attention or opportunity due to a lack of knowledge on the part of the public, or even the contractor, so the platform will also serve to increase the prominence of musicians of all musical styles, thus making them more relevant in the market. Especially in the Tatuí region, which is known as the city of music, training thousands of musicians through the various units of its conservatory, and also with the specialisation of musicians through the Phonographic Production course at FATEC Tatuí.

1.2 OBJECTIVES

1.3 GENERAL OBJECTIVE

The overall aim of this research project is to use information technology and digital marketing to develop career prospects for musicians and amateur bands by creating a web platform for publicising, hiring online and improving communication between client and applicant.

1.4 SPECIFIC OBJECTIVES

The specific objectives are:

a) Describe the lack of publicity for musicians and amateur bands;
b) Identify the requirements and the tools that will be used to solve the problem;
c) Using information technology to develop a tool to solve the problem;
d) Test and analyse the promotion of musicians and amateur bands using the tool developed with the project.

CHAPTER 2

THEORETICAL FRAMEWORK

2.1 HISTORY OF MUSIC

According to historical facts, music has been commonly manifested since the dawn of human life. Although music was an important activity among many ancient peoples, it was not considered an artistic activity. Its practice was linked to the various rituals that existed at that time, such as religion, birth, death, marriage, magic, war, mythology, etc. (PALISCA, 1988).

According to Palisca (1988), music emerged in the midst of the first civilisations that developed writing. Among the main civilisations were the Mesopotamians (Sumerians and Assyrians), Hebrews, Egyptians and Greeks.

According to Bona (PASQUALE BONA, 1816-1878), music is the art of expressing sounds and is divided into three elements: melody, harmony and rhythm.

The first polyphonic music appeared around the 9th century. Around this time composers began to experiment, introducing one or more lines of voices in order to add more beauty and refinement to their music. This style of music is called organum and the most widely used form of this style is the parallel organum, which is structured by two voices, the organ and the principal.

With the passing of the centuries and the advancement of harmony, music took on a more harmonically and rhythmically complex form. From the 18th century onwards, various composers such as Johann Sebastian Bach, Franz Joseph Haydn and others used the musical writing that is still the main one today, which uses melody, harmony and rhythms that are more elaborate than in previous centuries.

2.1.2 MUSIC CULTURE

2.1.3 MUSIC'S INFLUENCE ON SOCIETY

The Sumerians are the most culturally significant people of antiquity. Their culture flourished and influenced the world for over 3000 years.

Plato's work "The Republic" discusses a number of themes relating to man in society. In this same work, the great philosopher refers to the doctrine of "ETHOS", according to which music has the power to transform people's state of mind and control their actions. Plato (428 BC) and Aristotle (384 BC) defended music in education. For both of them, music represents the passions or states of the soul. They believed that education through music would contribute to the formation of a good individual. This individual, in turn, would contribute to the development of society.

From the 20th century onwards, music was no longer just used for cultural purposes, but became part of people's daily lives. The advance of technology led to a significant improvement in the dissemination of composers and musicians in general. By the 1960s, music was already an essential part of society: the number of music schools increased, music was played on the radio, in squares, at religious events, at social events, everywhere there was music.

2.2 BANDS AND MUSICAL GROUPS

At first, bands were formed in informal musical groups linked to military activity. In Ancient Egypt, Rome and the Middle East, we often find travelling musical groups, as in the Old Testament's biblical description of Joshua taking Jericho. Some historians say that banda is the feminine of bando, which comes from Latin and means flag. These musical groups marched with the flag at the front (PIMENTA, 2010).

Over the centuries and with the evolution of music in general, musical groups and bands have developed rapidly, making music one of the most coveted areas of work there is. Nowadays, this situation has diminished, thus putting a big damper on publicising and hiring in the music business, both for bands and musicians with solo careers.

2.3 MUSIC TODAY

2.3.2 CULTURAL REPRESENTATION OF MUSIC

Music is now considered the world's leading art form. From the Indians to the big cities, it is a strong artistic presence in local culture. The act of singing or listening to a song can trigger various emotional effects in a person. Sadness, joy, nostalgia, anger - many of these are the feelings that come over music listeners. These feelings, when contained in a large number of listeners, can generate social movements. For example, the punk, grunge, alternative and emo movements. Many movements sought, as a goal, greater freedom of expression and a better quality of life in society. (KOBYLINSKI, 2011)

The author goes on to say that music can therefore be considered one of the arts that has the most influence on society today, and for this reason the music market ended up becoming a market monopolised by the world's media. And as if music's main enemy was censorship, another major enemy has emerged: alienation.

> If we add this to the disregard for the quality of today's music in our country, especially for the less economically favoured classes, we can see a cultural decline. (KOBYLINSKI, 2011)

To complement this idea, Bueno (2013) states that music today is mostly used for dance. But it wasn't always like this; in dark times, even the sound of silence was enough to denounce the anguish that the country suffered in times of crisis and revolution. Music was once able to bring together crowds fighting for the same goal: freedom. The lack of technology was never an obstacle for those who used song as protest, music didn't need instruments, clapping whistles and cries were enough to form music in the hearts of those who struggled to survive from day to day.

As a very powerful cultural product, music has reached the present day with very different characteristics from what can be seen historically in Brazil. The changes are notable; today, with content intended only to give pleasure to the body through dance, music seems to have somewhat lost all its potential, but these changes are not the fault of the song, but rather its creator, with the aim of reaching the largest possible audience, and reaching the audience today is satisfied with just a dancing rhythm, caring less about its content and even less about its primary function. (BUENO, 2013)

Nowadays there are countless musical genres with countless purposes, from being just a dance beat to passing on a message, the main highlight of music is its ability to become global, making such a message capable of passing around the world. This makes the artist much more recognisable than other forms of art, and the number of bands, groups and musicians on the rise tends to grow considerably.

Figure 1 - Korean group TWICE, created in 2015, is already recognised worldwide and the winner of numerous awards.

But no matter how many transformations and influences there are, music never stops being music. Paiva (1992) gives the example that even with all the evolution and technologies that have been applied to the creation process, profoundly altering the whole "artistic process", this ends up becoming irrelevant - after all, the result is still music. There is no set rule or recipe for creating music, because each artist has their own way of creating it and they do it in the way that suits them, using the knowledge and technology at their disposal in different ways and forms, but in the end the result is the same.

2.3.2 THE MUSIC MARKET

The music business is full of professionals. According to Sebrae (2015), the music market is currently made up of authors, artists, technicians, producers, entrepreneurs, freelance professionals, as well as the media. There are organisations that supply products and services, bodies and inspection sectors. This whole network of people, products, services and processes, as well as the public that consumes it, is called the music market, a clean industry that doesn't pollute (apart from noise pollution) but generates income and thousands of jobs every day. It is possible to categorise the music market as a kind of ecosystem where points such as show business, the recording industry and copyright relate to internal market factors such as customers, competitors, collaborators and suppliers, as well as interacting with external forces such as technology, the economy, politics and society. (SEBRAE, 2015)

Figura 2 - The "ecosystem" of the music market

Source: SEBRAE (2015)

With the rapid evolution of technology, the music market has had to adapt at the same speed. According to Gonzales (2016), the rapid advance of technology has had a strong impact on the music market, and with the arrival of the internet, consumers are increasingly using online services, currently the largest online music shop in the world is part of Apple, the iTunes Store. The problem is that this service is paid for, which makes consumers look for alternative solutions so that they can access the same product without having to pay for it. In addition to this problem, there is a major obstacle to overcome: competition.

The author adds that the iTunes Store, which even with these obstacles dominated the market, has seen its position threatened by various streaming services. One example of great competition is Spotify, whose differential is that its content is free, with only adverts between songs. Google Play is also free for 30 days, as are Groove Music, TIDAL and Deezer, which also share the same differential. All offer access to more than 30 million songs. But in order to adapt, in June 2015 Apple introduced Apple Music, a streaming service similar to those mentioned above. As a result, the digital music market saw a 93% increase in consumption and a 45% increase in turnover.

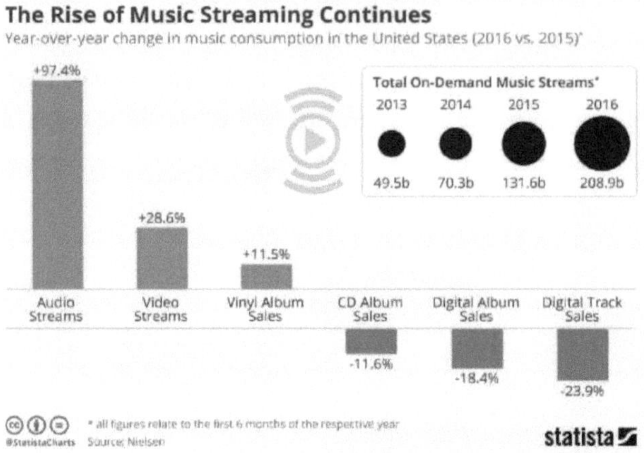

Figura 3 - The Music Streaming Market

Source: SEBRAE (2015)

In other words, this shows that the sheer competitiveness of this market means that suppliers have to adapt quickly and incorporate technological measures into music, both in its recording and in the way it is distributed and transmitted to the consumer. What's more, when it comes to music as a final consumer good, it's necessary, just like any other market, to identify the target audience in order to make the offer more attractive to its consumers.

2.3.3 GLOBAL AND REGIONAL OPPORTUNITIES IN MUSIC

According to Sebrae (2015) in Brazil, business opportunities are distributed across 14 economic activities, which are directly linked to the music industry, according to the National Classification of Economic Activities (CNAE), covering phonographic, copyright and show business activities, covering all stages of the production chain: formation, production, distribution, promotion, commercialisation and exhibition of musical goods or services. They are:

a) Sound reproduction on any medium;
b) Manufacture of musical instruments, parts and accessories;
c) Retail trade specialising in musical instruments and accessories;
d) Retail trade in discs, CDs, DVDs and tapes;
e) Sound recording and music editing;
f) Radio activities;
g) Internet portals and content providers;
h) Artistic agency and management;

i) Teaching music;

j) Music production;

k) Sound and lighting activities;

l) Art shows and cultural events;

m) Management of venues for performing arts, shows and other artistic activities;

n) Discos, discos, dance halls and the like

CNAE	Name	Activities covered	Qty
1830-0/01	Sound reproduction on any medium	Sound reproduction services on any medium from original recordings (matrices)	146
3220-5/00	Manufacture of musical instruments, parts and accessories.	Manufacture of pianos, organs, pianolas, stringed, wind, percussion and electronic musical instruments, music boxes, whistles, conductors' batons, metronomes and the like	780
4756-3/00	Retail trade specialising in musical instruments and accessories.	Retail trade in musical instruments, accessories and printed music.	5.770
4762-8/00	Retail sale of discs, CDs, DVDs and tapes.	Retail sale of discs, audio tapes, videos, CDs and DVDs - recorded or not.	8.626
5920-1/00	Sound recording and music editing activities.	This subclass includes: a) The recording of original matrices for sound reproduction on any medium and for any purpose, including advertising: b) The activity of reproducing, promoting and distributing recordings of musical compositions to the wholesale and retail trade or directly to the public. These activities may or may not be integrated with the production of original masters in the same unit. If not, the unit carrying out these activities must obtain the reproduction and distribution rights from the record company of the original masters; c) the activities of promoting and authorising musical compositions in recordings, on radio, on television, in films, in live performances and in other media. The units linked to these activities may own the copyright or act as music copyright administrators on behalf of the owners of these rights; d) recording services in studios or other locations, including the production of radio programmes to be broadcast at a later date; e) sound mixing services for recorded material; f) mastering and remastering services for sound material; g) the publishing of music and musical scores.	2.861
6010-1/00	Radio activities	This subclass also includes the broadcasting of radio programmes via the internet (internet radio stations).	3.049
6319-4/00	Portals, content providers and other information services on the Internet	This subclass also includes: A) services that make music available over the internet; B) access to programmes on the internet; C) e-mail services; D) advertising pages on the internet.	7.492
7490-1/05	Professional agency for sports, cultural and artistic activities.	Activities carried out by agencies or agents on behalf of individuals in order to obtain contracts to act in films, plays and other cultural, artistic and sporting performances.	278
8592-0/03	Teaching music.	This subclass comprises institutions that offer independent	10.247

		courses with musical instrument or singing teaching activities. This subclass also includes music lessons given by independent instructors of musical instruments or singing and the activity of music conservatories, with the exception of undergraduate courses.	
9001-9/02	Music production.	This subclass includes: a) the production activities of bands, musical groups, orchestras and other musical companies; b) concerts and operas; c) the activities of independent musicians. This subclass also includes; a) musical arrangement production; b) score composition activity; c) music production activity; d) organisation and promotion of a musical event (concert); e) independent musical theatre activity; f) trio elétrico activity.	27.060
9001-9/06	Sound and lighting activities.	This subclass includes sound and lighting activities for music halls, theatres and other spaces dedicated to artistic and cultural activities. This subclass also includes: a) sound equipment activity with operator; b) sound supply for entertainment venues; c) stage lighting services; d) supply of big screen with operator; e) DJ and VJ activities.	13.999
9001-9/99	Performing arts, shows and complementary activities not specified above.	This subclass includes: a) the activities of directors, producers and entrepreneurs of live artistic events; b) the production and promotion of artistic performances and cultural events not specified above; c) the production of sound and light shows; d) the production of pyrotechnic shows; e) the activities of television and radio programme presenters; f) the activities of writing scripts for theatre, cinema, etc...; g) set design activities.	7.608
9003-5/00	Management of venues for performing arts, shows and other artistic activities.	This subclass includes: a) the management of music halls, theatres and other artistic and cultural activities; b) the operation of entertainment venues; c) the management of cultural centres. This subclass also includes: a) operating theatre cafés; b) concert hall; c) showroom management activity.	326
9329-8/01	Discos, discos, dance halls and the like.	This subclass includes the activities of operating discos, nightclubs, cabarets, discos, dance halls, balls and similar activities (gafieiras, labateria, pagoda house, funk house, forró hall, etc.).	

Table 1 - Number of companies in the music industry, with an active CNPJ, opting for Simples Nacional, by CNAE, nationwide.

Source: SEBRAE (2015)

2.4 BUSINESS MANAGEMENT

2.4.1 CONTRACTS AND RECORD LABELS

The phonographic market is responsible for recording, distributing and commercialising musical media. With the arrival of the internet and the advent of the digital age, this segment felt the need to adapt. Nowadays, anyone can become a producer of content, including music. The internet has made it easier to publish these works, leading to financial and market independence, since artists can do without music producers, contracts with record companies and even performances on radio and television. Technological evolution has therefore led to the emergence of a new type of artist with no ties to record companies or third parties to launch themselves using the traditional model.

According to Santos et al. (2016), in the past, producing and recording discs required a high financial investment. All distribution required a mix of lobbying at points of sale, a complex logistics structure and frequent contact with the media. For the consumer, getting hold of the industry's products also occasionally required high investments. With the changes, everything that had previously been commercialised and difficult to access began to be distributed for free or for much lower prices through virtual formats such as MP3.

In addition to producing and promoting their products, in this case music, one of the functions of record companies is to manage the copyright protection of their branded products, to manage artists and their repertoires and, above all, to maintain their contracts with artists and their agents.

Santos et al. (2016) define a contract as a lawful legal transaction involving two or more parties who agree on a certain object or service, even if the parties have opposing interests. According to current Brazilian legislation and in line with the concept presented, it is clear that a contract is fundamentally the existence of two or more people who agree on certain clauses, and thus express a kind of agreement of wills on a certain interest.

The author states that a good example of an artistic contract, in addition to the signatures of the contracted party, the contracting party and two witnesses, should contain:

a) CONTRACTING PARTY

(Company), with registered office at (Rua), (número), (bairro), (CEP), (Cidade), (Estado), enrolled in the CNPJ under No. xxxxxx, and in the State Register under No. xxxxx, hereby represented by (Name), (nacionalidade), (civil estado), (profissão), bearer of identity card R.G. n° xxxxxx, and CPF/MF n° xxxxxx, resident and domiciled at (Street), (number), (neighbourhood), (postcode), (City), (State);

b) CONTRACTOR

(Name), (nationality), (marital status), (profession), bearer of identity card R.G. no. xxxxxxx and CPF/MF no. xxxxxxx, resident and domiciled at (Street), (number), (postcode), (City), (State).

c) THE OBJECT OF THE CONTRACT

Clause 1ª . The OBJECT of this contract is for the artist (xxxxxxxxxx), represented by the CONTRACTED PARTY, to give a performance of (Describe the type of performance to be given), at the place (xxx), on the day (xxx), starting at (xxx) o'clock and ending at (xxx) o'clock.

d) OBLIGATIONS

Clause 2a. It is the CONTRACTING PARTY's responsibility to provide the necessary permits and licences from the competent bodies for the execution of the artistic performance, and is also responsible for the accommodation, transport and food of the artist and his team of (xx) members.

e) THE EVENT

Clause 3ª . The CONTRACTED PARTY must arrive at the venue (xx) hours in advance to carry out the activities set out in this instrument. The CONTRACTING PARTY will provide all the sound and light equipment necessary for the musical performance, undertaking to respect the time necessary for the sound to be played (stipulate minimum time) and the fundamental conditions for the proper functioning of the CONTRACTED PARTY's equipment.

f) DATE TRANSFER

Clause 4a. If, for reasons of force majeure, the CONTRACTING PARTY requests a transfer of the date set above, it must inform the CONTRACTED PARTY at least (XX) days in advance. If, for reasons of force majeure, the CONTRACTED PARTY is unable to make the presentation, it must inform the CONTRACTING PARTY at least (XX) days in advance.

g) REMUNERATION

Clause 5a: The CONTRACTING PARTY shall pay the sum of R$ xxxxx (express amount) for the performance of the contracted artist, in two instalments, the first of which, in the amount of (xxx), shall be paid at the time of signing this contract. The second instalment will be due on the date of the event and must be paid before the artist takes the stage.

h) THE ARTIST'S NEEDS

Clause 6a: The CONTRACTING PARTY will make the following items available in the artist's dressing room: (Describe. E.g. water, food, sockets)

i) RESCISSION

Clause 7a: This contract will be cancelled if one of the parties fails to comply with the terms of this instrument. Clause 8a: In the event of any impediment to the event taking place, due to unforeseeable circumstances or force majeure, the parties must agree on another date or refund the amounts and replace what was spent on preparations.

j) Fines

Clause 9a. The party not in breach of any of the clauses set out in this instrument shall be compensated by the party giving rise to the breach, and a fine of (xx%) of the amount stipulated in clause 5a shall apply.

h) FORUM

Clause 10a The parties elect the jurisdiction of the district of (City) to settle any disputes arising from the CONTRACT.

2.4.2 THE INFORMAL MARKET

Informality in the Brazilian labour market and in several other countries is at a high level, and this has generated intense debate in society and in economic literature about the informal labour market. In Brazilian society, there is concern about the growing level of informality and its impact on social security accounts, for example (CURI; MENEZES, 2006).

Ulyssea (2005) states that Brazil's labour market has been characterised by a high proportion of workers without formal employment contracts since the 1980s. In 1981, according to the National Household Sample Survey (Pesquisa Nacional por Amostra de Domicílios - PNAD), a body belonging to the Brazilian Institute of Geography and Statistics (IBGE), 28% of the employed population did not have a formal work permit. The author adds that although this figure grew slightly in the first three years of the 1980s, the level of informality remained relatively stable throughout this period. However, from 1990 onwards there was an unprecedented rise in the level of informality in Brazilian labour, causing an increase of 10% by the end of 1990.

In Brazil, this problem has been reduced to a large extent because legislation now requires all workers who receive a salary to have a **signed labour card, which has led to the term "informal work" being** associated with whether or not the worker has a signed labour card. On an equal footing, in various works, informality is defined as the sum of workers without a signed labour card or who are self-employed, or even as the group of workers who do not contribute to social security. It can be concluded that, even if the problem is not so great, there is still a lack of organisation and dispersal of the literature, which makes it necessary to look for ways to turn previously informal work into something formal, in order to avoid a possible disparity between the lifestyles and salaries of both types of workers (ULYSSEA, 2005).

Even with all this pejorative tone, according to Nunes (2017), the latest data shows that unemployment has stopped rising, although this may seem like a good thing, if you analyse it in detail the main reasons for this slowdown are the

precariousness and giving up the search for employment may be the cause of these figures.

According to the IBGE (Brazilian Institute of Geography and Statistics), the unemployment rate reached 12.6 per cent in the third quarter of 2017, a reduction of 0.7 per cent compared to the previous quarter (March-April-May), when it stood at 13.3 per cent. Compared to July, the drop was 0.2 per cent. These figures are part of the National Household Sample Survey (PNAD). Compared to the same quarter of the previous year (2016), the figures are still up 0.8 per cent. In other words, there are still 13.1 million people looking for a job, 9.1 per cent more than in 2016, but 4.8 per cent more than in the third quarter of 2017.

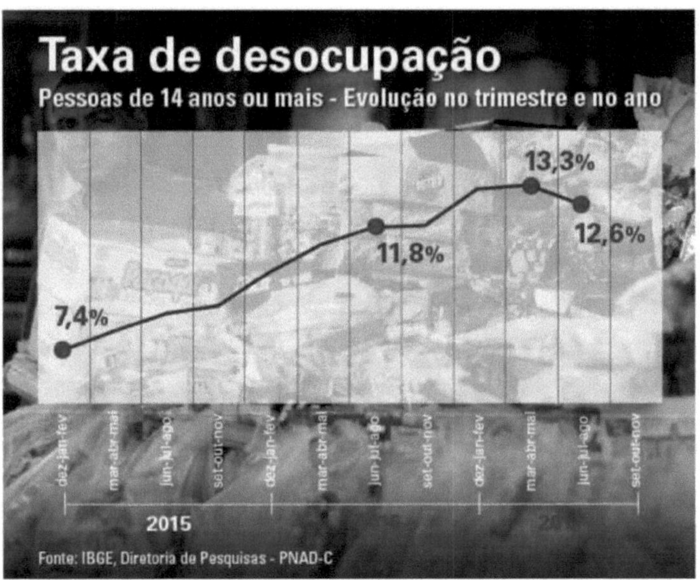

Figure 4 - Unemployment rate from the last quarter of 2015 to the third quarter of 2017. Source: REDACTION (2017)

2.5 MARKETING CONCEPTS

Marketing concepts were mistakenly understood simply as advertising and publicity, but today the complexity and evolution of this area is common knowledge. The conceptualisation of marketing

is wide-ranging and other factors are also involved besides advertising (STECCA; ÁVILA, 2015).

The authors state that a good understanding of marketing requires knowledge of three basic pillars:

a) Product - a product is understood to be anything that can satisfy a consumer need or desire. A product can be considered to be either a physical object or a service;

b) Barter - is simply the act of transacting, i.e. where a product or service is exchanged for money;

c) Market - the market is considered to be the place where transactions take place, anywhere there is a potential for trade there is a market, the market can be segmented by product, location, age and so on.

> Marketing involves delivering value to the customer, and when we use the term value in marketing it doesn't just mean the price to pay for the product, but also the benefits that this product or service provides to those who buy it.

Marketing is therefore defined as a set of techniques and methods aimed at improving sales, using possibilities such as price, distribution, communication and product. In a general sense, it is the understanding of business policy, where the development of sales plays an important role. With the arrival of new technologies, marketing is receiving more space and opening up the possibility of devising new strategies. This possibility is defined by digital marketing, which consists of a set of strategic actions applied to digital media such as the internet, mobile, e-commerce, among others, to build customer loyalty and increase the company's market share.

1.1.1 EVOLUTION OF MARKETING

Cappellari et al. (2016) say that over the years, the world market has undergone significant changes in terms of the behavioural aspect of the

The author goes on to say that over the years and following Philip Kotler's philosophy, marketing has evolved, and with this evolution the focus of marketing managers has changed. Marketing 1.0 was focused on the product and in the evolution to 2.0 the focus shifted to the consumer, and in 3.0 the focus shifted from the consumer to the human being themselves, where all profitability must be balanced by corporate responsibility, which then came to be called values marketing.

The evolution of marketing

Analyse	Marketing 1.0	Marketing 2.0	Marketing 3.0
	Product-centred	Consumer-centred	Aimed at Values
Objective	Selling products	Satisfying and retaining customers	Making the world a better place
Trigger	Industrial Revolution	Information Technology	New wave of

			technology
Customer vision	Mass buyers with physical needs.	Consumers Intelligent, with a heart and a mind.	Full human being, with heart, mind and spirit.
Concept of Marketing	Product development	Differentiation	Values
Guidelines for Marketing	Product specification	Product and company positioning	Company mission, vision and values
Value Proposition	Functional	Functional and emotional	Functional, emotional and spiritual
Interaction with consumers	One-to-one transaction	One-to-one relationship para-one	One-to-many collaboration.

Table 2 - Evolution of marketing from 1.0 to 3.0 Source: Adapted from Cappellari et al. (2016)

2.5. 2DIGITAL MARKETING

MARTINS (2010) says that with the rapid growth of the internet, it has become one of the best means of communication, information distribution and research. The internet has radically affected all areas of knowledge, especially marketing, with the advantages of being accessible, cheap and able to work in conjunction with traditional marketing.

COSTA et al. (2015) adds that digital marketing is a means of facilitating the purchase and sale of a product or service. Through the internet, managers are able to work globally, news emerges quickly, because it is highly accessible, it makes interactivity even more present, through social networks it is possible to provide such interactivity (SANTOS, 2014).

SANTOS (2014) goes on to say that interaction is fundamental to marketing in the virtual environment. Digital media make the relationship between the customer and the seller much easier on the internet, not just in terms of customer service. The internet helps to take marketing to the next level, as it facilitates the collection of customer data, making it possible for companies to set up strategies according to their market niche.

> Knowing the consumer's profile makes it possible to plan actions that will be within the context of the moment, the brand and the customer themselves. In other words, as mentioned above, digital marketing not only builds customer loyalty, helps measure results and responds quickly to feedback, but is also based on good relationships, which will be crucial to defining successful strategies (SANTOS 2014).

The growth in the number of users on the World Wide Web and in e-commerce has aroused the interest of Internet marketers. Under these conditions, the Internet has become one of the largest means of buying and selling there is, but in order to gain prominence in this gigantic world of the Internet, it is necessary to devise global strategies so that you can bring synergy to a particular source of business in partnership with your sales objectives, reaching your target market through appropriate advertising (SILVA, 2009).

With this in mind, Silva (2009) says that the internet can bring unique benefits to marketing, one of which is the low cost of distributing information to the public, and the interactive nature of the internet.

Internet marketing, both for the instantaneous provision of answers to customers and for obtaining answers from consumers.

1.1.3 MUSIC MARKETING

With the unbridled growth of the internet, there have been radical changes in various sectors of industry and commerce, one of which is the music business. Many bands use the internet to expand their image in the market, which helps them to be recognised and makes it easier to get hired.

Marketing actions in music are developed through clinical and continuous processes, so before being launched onto the market, it is extremely important to plan calmly and effectively. These analyses should tell you what prices you are aiming for and what prices the market can offer you, what the means of promotion will be and what tactics you should use (BARBOSA, 2014).

With the internet and social networks, artists have gained greater accessibility and it is vital to maintain the relationship between audience and fan. Artists can use countless strategies, tools and applications to reach their audience and generate this relationship. CAPPELLATO (2014) says that you shouldn't just take photos and post them online, it's important to work on the band's image through music marketing strategies and thus optimise the relationship with fans.

2.6 THE HISTORY OF THE INTERNET

Before talking about web programming, we need to talk about how the internet came about, why without the internet there would be no websites, e-commerce and this degree programme.

Bisneto (2003) states that the starting point for the creation of the internet was the launch of the first communication satellite by the USSR in 1957, Sputnik, where in the same year another satellite of the same name was launched, Sputnik 2, where the first living terrestrial being was launched into space, the dog Laika, and from then on the space race between the USA and the USSR began.

MEYER (2014) adds that the Internet emerged for military purposes during the Cold War, with the aim of interconnecting US bases to ensure communication between bases even if enemy attacks destroyed the means of communication that already existed at the time. The first version of the Internet, ARPANET, worked with a packet switching system, where information was divided into mini packets.

Between the 1970s and 1980s, the world was calm, with no immediate attack imminent. The US government allowed researchers to develop studies at their universities using ARPANET, making it a great means of academic communication. Through it, students and professors, mostly from the USA, exchanged ideas, messages and discoveries while they were still in their infancy (MEYER, 2014).

KLEINA (2011) concludes by saying that over the years and with the gradual increase in users and the weakening of the Cold War, the ARPANET lost its military character, but due to its great potential, in 1983 the MILNET was created, which would serve only for the war and the scientific functions would be the responsibility of the ARPANET, which in 1989 had the greatest development, serving as the basis for several networks connected to each other, giving rise to the Internet.

2.7 IT SUPPORT FOR COMMUNICATION

For a long time, IT was considered just a support item for the organisation, just a "cost centre" that initially didn't generate any kind of return for the business. But over the years, IT applications have grown in organisations. While technology used to be used only to automate tasks and eliminate human labour, it has gradually begun to add much more to the entire organisational process, helping to optimise activities, eliminate communication barriers and much more. (SANTOS, 2009)

Straliotto (2016) adds that in a scenario of real-time communication such as social networks and especially mobile technology, we end up facing ever greater challenges, where we live with the latent need to present something new to an audience that is currently seen as anxious and curious, but at the same time is saturated with too much information. In addition to exploring creativity, there is a need to analyse the tools already known to make a campaign happen.

The author uses Brainstorming as an example, where there is a great idea, but then the question arises: but how to do it? Then people realise that knowledge isn't always enough for an idea to come to life. And in the midst of so much technology, someone capable of solving these problems emerges: the Information Technology professional.

When it comes to communication, today it is developed, stored and made available on the internet, allowing the public to access it from anywhere, according to their needs. While employees think about how best to present this content and interact with it. IT professionals analyse how to make the offers operational and technical.

Communication is therefore extremely important for all sectors to work together, improving the quality and efficiency of the development, monitoring and finalisation of a project, and IT has the necessary tools for this communication to be successfully implemented.

2.8 LEGISLATION

2.8.1 COPYRIGHT

The Central Office of Collection and Distribution Ecad (2010) defines copyright as a set of prerogatives granted by law to the individual or legal entity that is the creator of the intellectual work, so that they can enjoy both the moral and patrimonial benefits resulting from the exploitation of their creations. Copyright is regulated by the Copyright Law (Law 9.610/98) and protects the relationship between the creator and those who use their artistic, literary or scientific creations, such as texts, books, paintings, sculptures, music, photographs, etc. Copyright is divided into two for legislative purposes: moral rights and property rights.

Moral rights secure the authorship of the creation to the author of the work, in which case the works are protected by copyright. Property rights, on the other hand, are primarily concerned with the economic utilisation of the intellectual work. It is the author's exclusive right to use their creative work in any way they wish, as well as to allow third parties to use it, in whole or in part.

In contrast to moral rights, which cannot be transferred or waived, property rights can be transferred or assigned to other people, but the author can allow the right of representation or even the use of their creations. If the intellectual work is used without any kind of prior authorisation, the person responsible for such unauthorised use will be in breach of copyright rules, and their conduct could lead to legal action. (ECAD, 2010)

2.9 DEVELOPMENT TOOLS

2.9.1 THE PHP LANGUAGE (HYPERTEXT PREPROCESSOR)

The PHP language is one of the most widely used on the web. According to NIEDERAUER (2011), the language is already used on millions of websites. Its difference from other existing languages is PHP's high capacity to interact with the web, completely changing websites that use static pages.

In terms of maintenance, control and distribution, LOPES et al. (2017) states that there is the PHP Group. This group is made up of several professionals in the field living in various parts of the world, providing support, producing documentation and distributing it so that other professionals can have access to the language. All this support is free and has been produced in several languages and can be accessed from the group's website.

ARAUJO (2009) states that PHP has several advantages besides the fact that it is free, it is multiplatform, i.e. it works not only in the Windows environment, but also on other systems such as Linux, Unix, FreeBSD and others, with this advantage it is possible to transfer scripts from one machine to another without the need to change the code just by making the transfer. In addition to these, the author cites other advantages such as easy learning, since it is a language made from "fragments" of other languages such as Pearl, Java and C, most developers who know one of these languages are already one step ahead. PHP is very easy to integrate with systems such as Sybase, MySQL, MS-SQL, Oracle and others compatible with the ODBC standard.

One of the biggest advantages of PHP is that it has open source code, due to the fact that many companies are against creating tools using Microsoft tools because they are tied to the company and there is no access to the source code. Some companies need to be extremely careful with security and cannot blindly trust their fate to a single company. It is necessary to always be inspecting the source code to ensure that there are no security flaws that end up compromising the entire site (ARAUJO, 2009).

2.9.2 MYSQL

According to NIEDERAUER (2005), MySQL is a database management system that uses SQL (Structured Query Language), created in Sweden by David Axmark, Allan Larsson and Michael "Monty" Widenius in the 1980s.

MySQL arose from the need of the team that created the DBMS to use mechanisms to connect tables created in the SQL language. At first, the group was going to use a tool that they soon realised was not fast enough to meet the project's needs - this tool was mSQL. So they decided to create their own solution. So MySQL was born (NIEDERAUER 2005).

MySQL is a great tool for database development because, although it has complex database technology, its cost is very low and its features of speed, scalability and reliability stand out, making it widely used by web developers and software package vendors.

2.9.3 RESPONSIVENESS

Nowadays, when creating a website, it's becoming commonplace to think about developing for a mobile version. In addition to the various screen sizes on desktops, there are also different sizes on mobile devices, which makes it extremely complicated to build specific websites for each platform or device. (ALBAN et al., 2012)

In this context, ALBAN et al. (2012) demonstrates the need to find a solution that adapts to the user's environment and behaviour when accessing information, taking into account factors such as screen resolution, orientation and the platform the user is using.

According to TEIXEIRA (2011) the advantages of responsive design are:

a) Adapt the layout to practically any resolution that the website would be viewed in;

b) Saving mobile data by automatically resizing images;

c) Make navigation simpler, for situations where the user doesn't have time to absorb all the information on the screen;

d) Hide unnecessary elements on smaller devices;

e) Use mobile resources such as geolocalisation;

In short, the use of responsiveness has become fundamental to facilitating the user experience on all types of platforms, both desktop and mobile. It's possible to standardise the way pages are displayed in different browsers and achieve a pleasant look by defining our own formatting. (K19 TREINAMENTOS, 2013).

2.9.4 CSS (CASCADING STYLES SHEETS)

PEREIRA (2009) states that in order to talk about responsiveness, we must also talk about CSS, whose important function is to make the site responsive. CSS, like HTML, is not a programming language, but it is very important when it comes to web design.

CSS, as the acronym implies, is a style sheet language that aims to define how documents in the markup language (HTML or XML) will be presented in terms of formatting and layout, i.e. while HTML structures content, CSS formats it, making the two languages highly integrated. (PEREIRA, 2009)

LOPES and KOMURA (2011) state that it is extremely difficult to maintain readable code using only HTML. As a result, new ways of formatting pages emerged and with the large increase in TAGs in the language, the code ended up becoming more confusing and incompatible with the browsers of the time. With this in mind, CSS was created with the intention of making the use of HTML more practicable with the aim of only taking care of the style of the page. With the advantage of being more robust than HTML in terms of styling.

CHAPTER 3

MATERIALS AND METHODS

3.1 MATERIALS AND INSTRUMENTS

a) Computer;
b) Mobile phone;
c) Internet access, either via network connection or mobile data;
d) Notepad++, source code editor;
e) PHP is a free interpreted language used to develop server-side applications;
f) MYSQL is a database management system that uses the SQL language as its interface).
g) PHPMYADMIN is a free, open-source web application developed in PHP for administering MySQL over the Internet;
h) HTML (HyperText Markup Language) is a markup language used to build web pages. HTML documents can be interpreted by browsers.
i) CSS (Cascading Style Sheets) is a mechanism for adding style (colours, fonts, spacing, etc.) to a web document;
j) JAVASCRIPT is an interpreted programming language. It was implemented as part of web browsers;

3.2 PEOPLE

3.3 TECHNICAL PROCEDURES

The technical procedures for the development of this project were: using the PHP language to programme the system for publicising musicians and bands, using the MySQL database to store the data on the web page and using the CSS language with the bootstrap framework to make the web page adaptable to mobile devices. The system has a home page with several adverts for musicians or bands, each with a star rating system made by users and contractors of the musical services. A registration/login system so that the data to be entered on the page is secure.

The website was developed through research into the shortcomings suffered by bands and amateur musicians when it comes to publicising their work. After this analysis, the process of building the **"DivulgaSom"** website will begin. The development of the web platform will take place according to the schedule drawn up, as well as periodic and constant testing. Therefore, the technical procedures adopted for the project were:

a) Initial tests of the site have been carried out by musicians and/or bands who wish to use the platform on their personal computers

b) NotePad++ is a multiplatform text editing software that will be used to develop and edit source code;

c) PHPmyadmin together with MySQL is a database management system (DBMS) that uses SQL (Structured Query Language) as its interface;

d) HTML (HyperText Markup Language) will be used as the standard for the structured representation of the screens and colours of the application and its usability in prototyping;

e) CSS (Cascading Style Sheets) one of the code editor extensions used to standardise application pages;

f) JAVASCRIPT, will provide the application's pages with the possibility of new programming and processing of data sent and received, interacting with the markup and display of HTML language content and with the stylisation of this content provided by CSS on these pages;

g) The server that will be used to store the site's data in the cloud will be Hostinger and the intended domain will be: divulgasom.net.br

3. 4PROTOTYPING

To develop the screens for the prototype, we used the printscreen screen capture mode available on all computers and smartphones and the Paint software, a freely available image creation programme for Windows.

This section will present the site's screens, starting with the registration page, which was initially created to register a minimum number of musicians to be publicised on the site's actual home page.

Figure 5 - interface of the registration homepage of the www.divulgasom.xyz site (where it is currently hosted). (Modified bootsrap template)

On this initial registration page, we collect the personal details of the musician or band leader, such as full name, date of birth, e-mail address and password, for future access to the site.

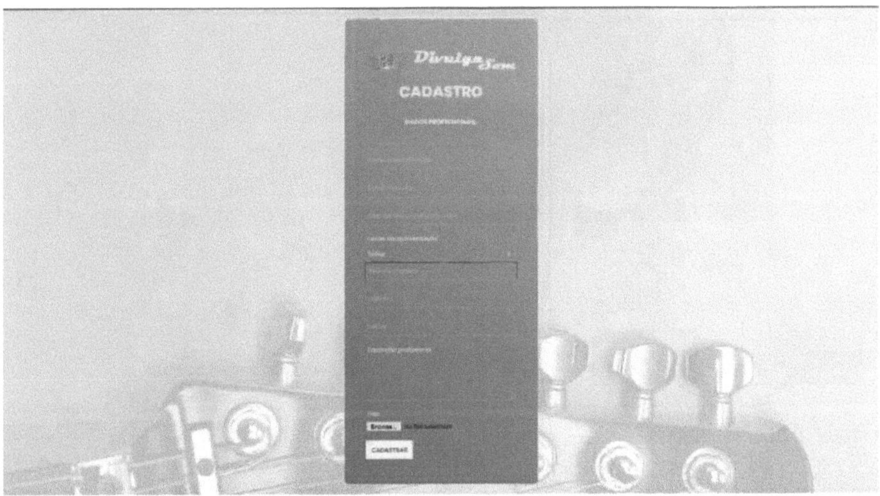

Figure 6 - Interface of the site's second registration page

In the next stage of registration, you'll be asked to enter your details, such as: artist/band name, musical styles, cities available for you to play in, venues you can choose from: weddings, bars, parties, or a solo musician in case a band wants to hire you to take part, city, state, professional description, and a photo to be published on the site.

Figure 7 - Interface of the site's third registration page

The last stage, a thank you for registering and a message saying: Your profile will be analysed and published on Divulga Som soon.

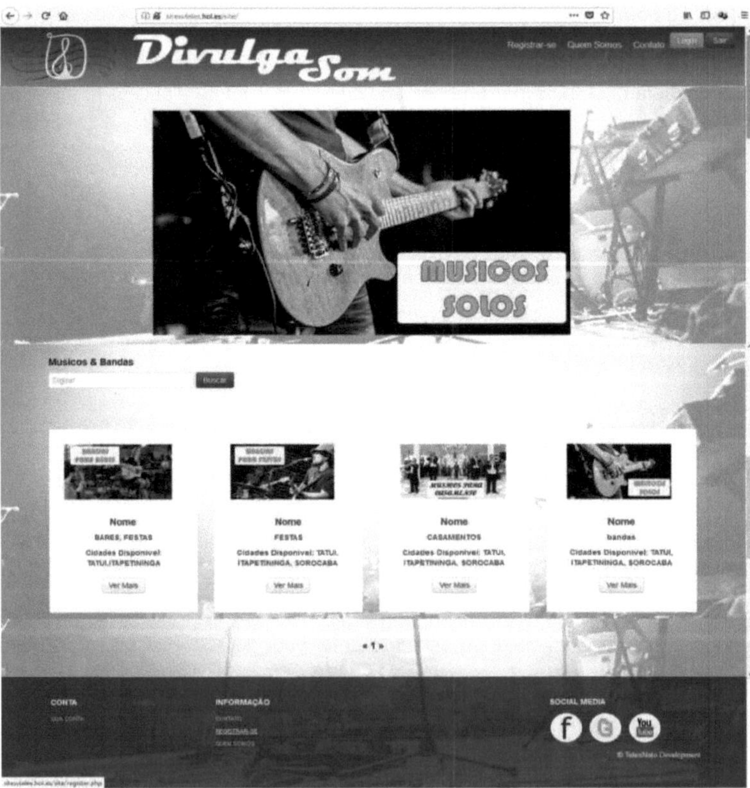

Figure 8 - Website homepage interface

This main screen shows all the musicians and bands registered, with information on their stage names, venues where they perform, and cities available for possible events.

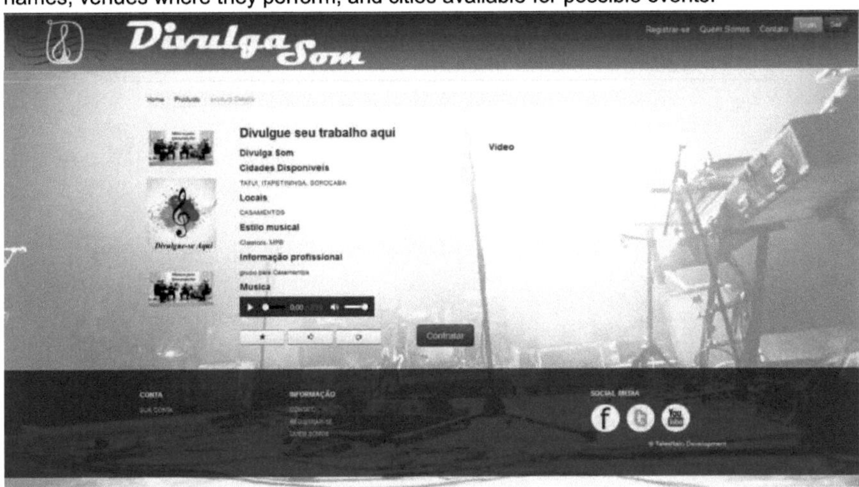

Figure 9 - Interface of the individual information page for each Musician/Band.

This screen shows all the information about the chosen musicians or band, such as their name, stage name, cities available for performances, venues, musical styles, professional information, photos, a song and a link to a video.

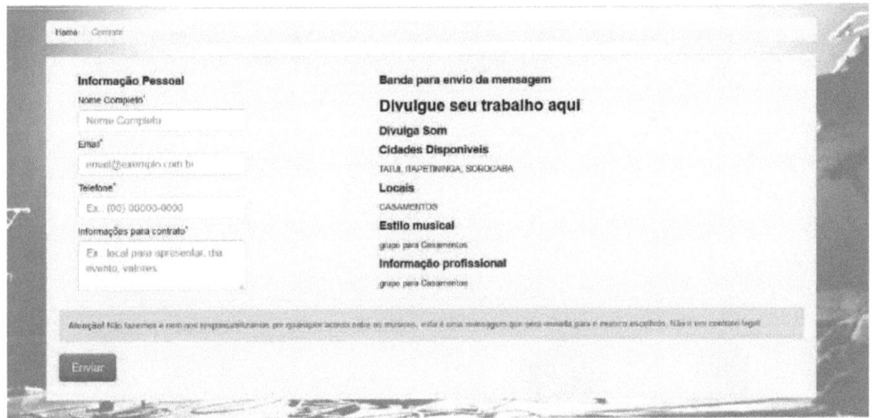

Figure 10 - Interface of the chosen musician's contract page.

Once you have clicked on Hire, you are directed to this screen where you can send a message to the chosen musician or band, this message will arrive at the registered musician's email address, and they will contact the contractor.

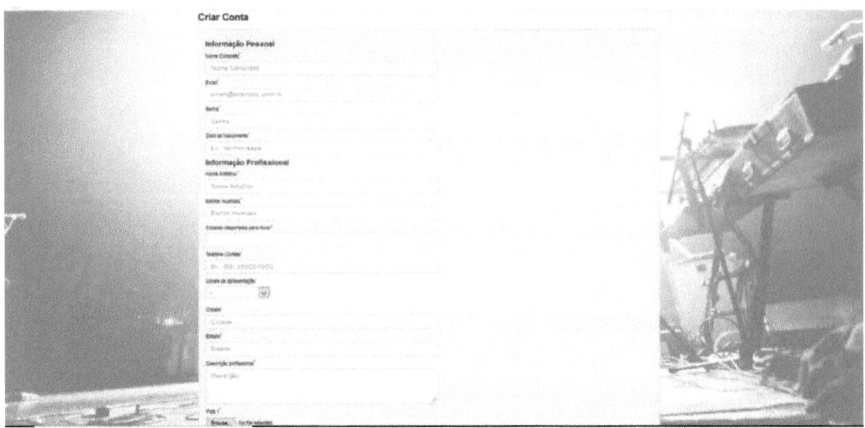

Figure 11 - Interface of the site's musician/band user registration page.

On the registration page, the musician's or band leader's personal details are obtained, such as full name, date of birth, e-mail address, and password for future access to the site, as well as the musician's or band's details, such as: stage name/band, musical styles, cities available to play in, venues, with the option of choosing some pre-defined ones: weddings, bars, parties, or a solo musician in case a band wants to hire them to take part, city, state, professional description, and a photo to be publicised on the site.

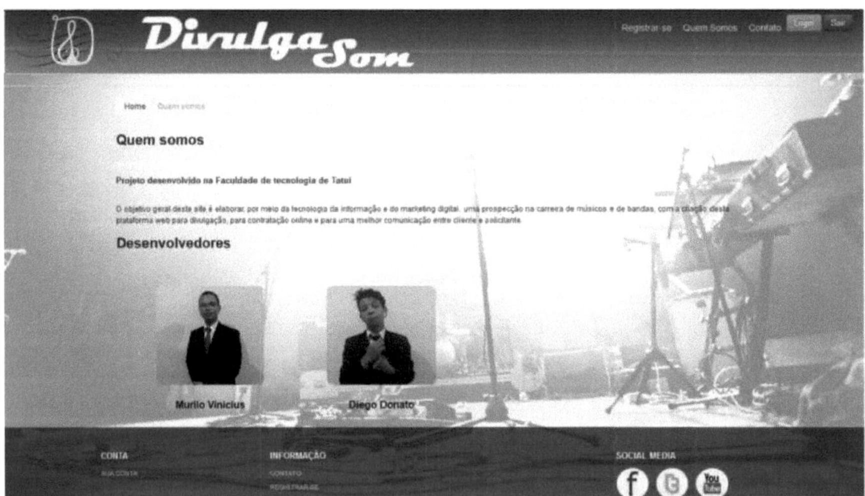

Figure 12 - Interface of the site's developer page.

This page gives a brief overview of these projects and their developers.

Figure 13 - Website contact page interface.

The contact page contains all the social networks created for the Divulgasom website, as well as a contact form for questions, suggestions, etc.

CHAPTER 4

RESULTS AND DISCUSSION

4.1.2 ANALYSING THE PLATFORM'S USABILITY

With regard to development time, five months were invested in working on this project, but all this time was due to bibliographical analyses of the subject under investigation. All the methods planned for implementing the system were successfully realised. As far as the programming of the site is concerned, it can be said that there has been a great deal of progress, and in almost three months the site was practically complete and already being used by the public.

4.1 ANALYSING THE PUBLIC

To analyse the site with the public, a questionnaire was carried out with some of the registered musician users, using the Google Docs tool, where a series of questions were asked about the experience of using the DivulgaSom site. The table below shows the data obtained from the questions, and the scores for each answer given, from 0 to 10 (0 being very bad and 10 being excellent).

Date stamp	Easy site registration.	Easy account management	Easy to find on the site (when searched)	Visual quality of the site	Would you recommend the site to a friend?
01/06/2018	10	8	7	7	Yes
04/05/2018	8	10	8	9	Yes
14/05/2018	7	9	8	8	Yes
10/05/2018	10	8	9	6	Yes
16/05/2018	9	10	7	10	Yes
04/05/2018	9	10	8	10	Yes
11/05/2018	9	8	10	9	Yes
04/05/2018	9	9	9	8	Yes
18/05/2018	10	10	10	10	Yes
15/05/2018	7	7	7	7	Yes
15/05/2018	9	4	7	9	Yes
30/05/2018	6	6	6	8	Yes
30/05/2018	5	3	7	9	Yes
04/05/2018	5	7	8	6	Yes
04/05/2018	7	8	6	6	Yes
12/05/2018	9	7	8	7	Yes
13/05/2018	10	7	9	9	Yes
11/05/2018	8	8	9	8	Yes
15/06/2018	7	6	4	7	Yes
14/06/2018	7	6	9	10	Yes
30/05/2018	9	7	7	7	Yes
16/06/2018	10	9	10	10	Yes

25/06/2018	10	8	8	7 Yes
17/05/2018	7	4	6	7 Yes
22/05/2018	9	8	7	8 Yes
20/06/2018	9	6	7	8 Yes

Table 3 - Questionnaire results.

Graphs were generated for each question, showing the results of the survey.

Facilidade no cadastro do site.

26 respostas

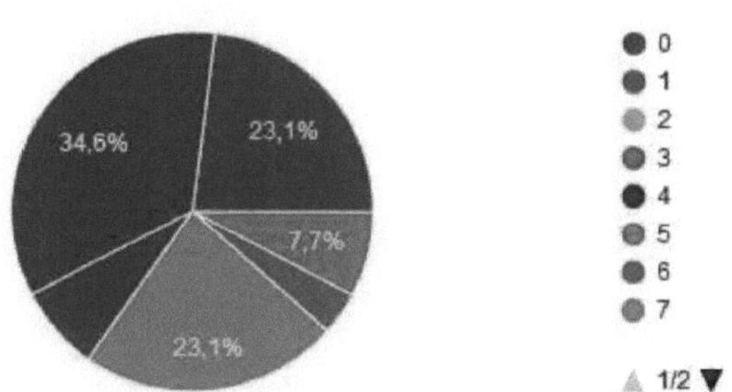

Figura 14 - Graph Ease of registering on the site.

The first question asks how easy it is to register a musician or band on the DivulgaSom website.

Facilidade no gerenciamento da conta

26 respostas

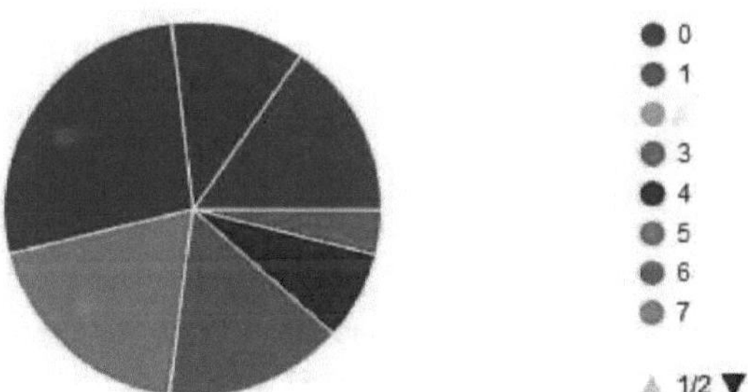

Figura 15 - Chart Ease of account management.

The next question is about how easy it is to manage the account. The data shows that there wasn't much approval for this part, not least because initially they couldn't access the account, as the site didn't yet have a minimum number of musicians registered for display

Facilidade em se encontrar no site (quando pesquisado)

26 respostas

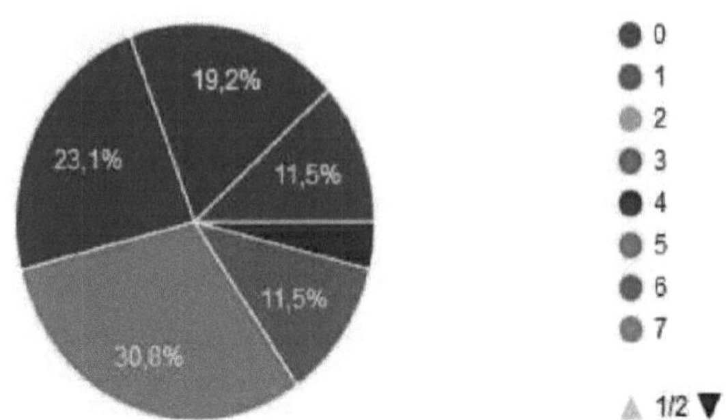

Figura 16 - Graph Ease of finding the site (when searched).

This question refers to how easy it is to find the page when searching, either by direct link or by searching on a search provider such as Google, Bing Yahoo and others.

Qualidade visual do site

26 respostas

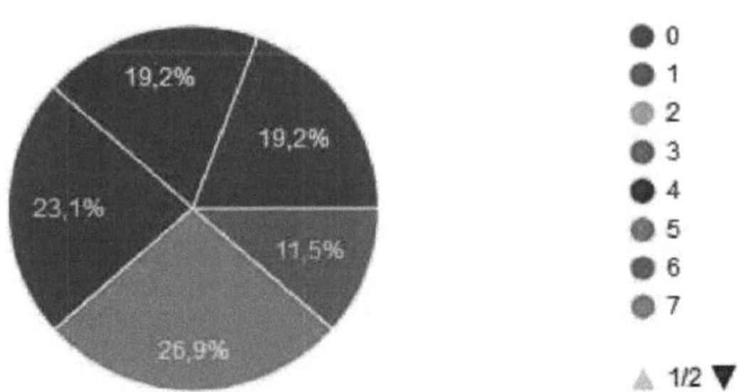

Figura 17 - Graphic Visual quality of the site.

The fourth question is about the visual quality of the site, whether it is intuitive and interactive with the user.

Figura 18 - Graphic Would you recommend the site to a friend?

And the last question in this questionnaire is whether the user would recommend this advertising platform to a friend, and we got 100% acceptance.

4.1.3 ANALYSING THE NEED FOR THE PLATFORM

For this form, the same Google Docs tool was used and the answers were given in the form of numbers from 1 (not very good) to 5 (very good) and the following questions related to the need for a music promotion platform and the user's expectations of the DivulgaSom platform:

a) Do you have experience with music promotion platforms?

b) What level of demand do you have for music promotion platforms?

c) How satisfied are you with these sought-after platforms?

d) Using the DivulgaSom platform, what rating would you give it?

e) Quantify your expectations regarding the contribution of the DivulgaSom... website;

The survey was carried out with a total of 13 musicians in addition to the others registered, and obtained the following results:

Do you have experience with music promotion platforms?

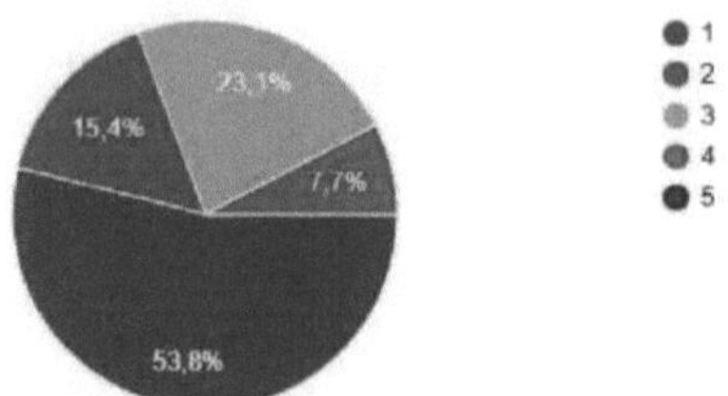

Figura 19 - Chart "**Do you have experience with** music **promotion platforms**?"

The graph above shows that many of the musicians interviewed have little or no experience with promotion platforms. This could be due to various factors, such as a lack of knowledge of these platforms, a lack of prominence in the market for these platforms or even informal ways of publicising the musician's work.

Qual seu nível de procura em relação à plataformas de divulgação musical?

Figure 20 - **Graph "What level of demand do you have for** music promotion **platforms**? "

This graph complements the previous one, showing that the demand for a promotion platform is low, or even non-existent. This may also be due to the limited availability of platforms on the market or those with a high profile, which leads to a lack of interest on the part of the musician in using these formal means of promotion.

Qual o seu grau de satisfação nessas plataformas já procuradas?

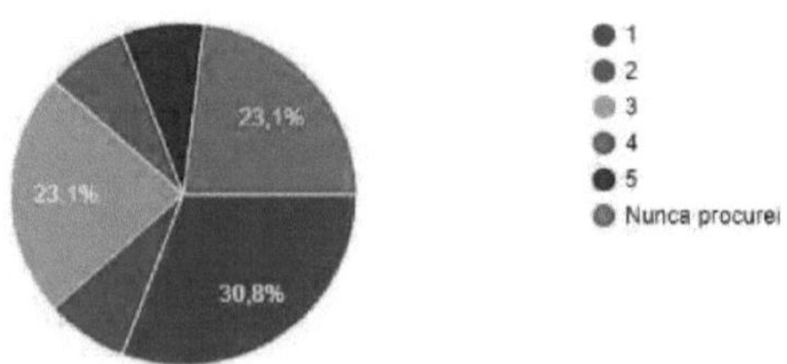

Figura 21 - Chart How satisfied are you with the platforms you've already used? "

This graph shows that the musicians who have had experience with this type of platform have not been satisfied with the platforms they have found. Some factors that could have influenced this are the lack of quality, difficulty of use or even the lack of feedback from the site in terms of hiring.

Utilizando a plataforma DivulgaSom, qual nota você atribui?

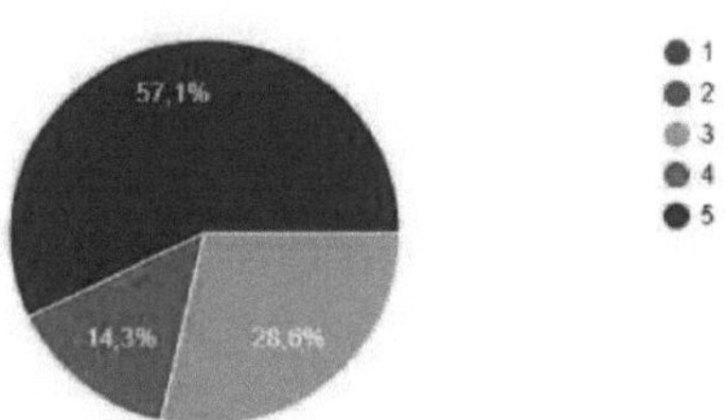

Figura 22 - **Chart "Using the DivulgaSom platform, what rating would you give it? "**

The graph shows the level of satisfaction with the DivulgaSom platform. This score can also be compared with the average taken from the previous questionnaire, based on the items also asked previously. This score will help us to make the necessary improvements to the platform, and also to develop DivulgaSom's values and mission in terms of entrepreneurship.

Quantifique suas expectativas em relação a contribuição do site DivulgaSom.

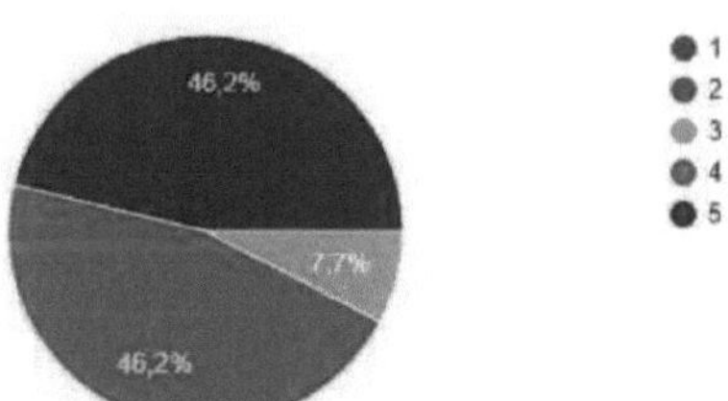

Figure 22 - **Graph "Using the DivulgaSom platform, what rating would you give it? "**

The musicians' expectations regarding the platform's contribution to their careers are high, due to the fact that the platform has a good niche in terms of location, as it is located in the city of Tatuí, known as the city of music, which covers a good part of the market segment and at the same time gives the platform a good edge.

FINAL CONSIDERATIONS

Considering the market's need for platforms to publicise musicians and amateur bands, DivulgaSom will be a great help in making life easier for musicians who have just started their careers. As for the platform, this is just the beginning, it is hoped that over time the platform will be constantly improved and that it can become a business with its own missions, visions and values, expanding its clients and becoming a reference in terms of promoting musicians. We intend to set up partnerships with clubs, pubs, bars and contractors in general so that as well as publicising musicians, we can also publicise those who need them, further increasing the platform's reach, We also have the future goal of implementing an online hiring system in partnership with third-party payment companies, thus facilitating hiring. In short, we still have many opportunities for evolution that, if well exploited, will make us grow even more in the market, both in the region and nationally, and even further afield, globally.

CHAPTER 5

CONCLUSION

The opportunity to be recognised for your work is a priceless feeling, and for those who can't get this recognition in an easy and agile way, the development of a publicity system is ideal for the promotion of anyone in society. The DivulgaSom platform is the result of a unique effort by the team, to make the work of musicians and amateur bands something formal and prominent in the market, making it capable of overcoming the small obstacle that is the lack of recognition when entering the industry, even with the various ways to carry out this publicity, the need for musicians to .

Based on the theories of marketing, studied in depth and objectively, and also on the practical application materials offered during the course, and complemented by the search for knowledge in other sources, this work seeks to help create this project, despite having a reach that is not yet so great, it is hoped that over time the platform will gain great prominence in the market, It is also hoped to expand the platform from a simple graduation project into a future business, using all the knowledge of entrepreneurship acquired during the course, thus enabling us to have a clinical eye for problem-solving and business management.

REFERENCES

ALBAN, Afonso et al. Expanding the usability of web interfaces for the elderly on mobile devices: a proposal using responsive design. 2012. Available at: <http://www.seer.ufrgs.br/index.php/renote/article/view/36404/23511 Accessed on: 21 Nov. 2017.

ARAUJO, Fabricio. ADVANTAGES AND DISADVANTAGES OF PHP. 2009. Available at: <https://www.inforlogia.com/vantagens-e-desvantagens-do-php/>. Accessed on: 13 Nov. 2017.

BARBOSA, Arthur. Music Marketing: How to apply marketing in the world of music? 2014. Available at : <http://www.ideiademarketing.com.br/2014/04/30/marketing-musical-como-aplicar-o- marketing-no-mundo-da-musica/>. Accessed on: 13 Nov. 2017.

BISNETO, Pedro Luiz O. Costa. The History of the Internet. 2003. Available at: <http://www.pedroom.com.br/portal/vitae/download/cientificos/03 A Historia da Internet.pdf>. Accessed on: 13 Nov. 2017.

BONA, Pasquale. METHOD OF THEORY AND SOLFEGGIO. Ricordi do Brasil .1816-1878.

BUENO, Erika de Souza. Today's music. 2013. Available at: <http://www.jb.com.br/sociedade-aberta/noticias/2013/01/14/as-musicas-de-hoje/>. Accessed on: 16 Apr. 2018.

BUENO, Erika de Souza. Today's music. 2013. Available at: <http://www.jb.com.br/sociedade-aberta/noticias/2013/01/14/as-musicas-de-hoje/>. Accessed on: 16 Apr. 2018.

CAPPELLARI, Gabriela et al. ANALYSIS OF MARKETING 1.0, 2.0 AND 3.0 AND THE COMPETITIVENESS LEVEL OF HOUSEHOLD APPLIANCES IN THE NORTHWEST OF

GAÚCHO: AN EXPLORATORY STUDY Gabriela CAPPELLARI1. 2016. Availableat : <file:///C:/Users/Dinhego/Downloads/ MARKETING ANALYSIS 10 20 e 30 E D O_NIVEL_DE_COMP.pdf>. Accessed on: 28 May 2018.

CAPPELLATO, Fred. Digital marketing in music. 2014. Available at: <http://cappellato.com.br/fotografia-e-o-marketing-digital-na-musica/>. Accessed on: 13 Nov. 2017.

COSTA, Lucas Mendes da et al. THE EVOLUTION OF DIGITAL MARKETING: A MARKET STRATEGY. 2015. Available at: <http://www.ufjf.br/facom/files/2014/03/Marketing-na-Era-Digital.pdf>. Accessed on: 11 Nov. 2017.

CURI, Andréa Zaitune; MENEZES, Naércio Aquino. Is the Brazilian labour market segmented? Changes in the profile of informality and wage differentials in the 1980s and 1990s. 2006. Available at: <http://www.scielo.br/scielo.php?pid=s0101-41612006000400008&script=sci_arttext>. Accessed on: 25 May 2018.

GONZALES, Erica. The music economy: the music services sector. 2016. Available at: <https://economiadeservicos.com/2016/09/06/a-economia-da- musica-o-sector-de-servicos-musicais/>. Accessed on: 16 Apr. 2018.

GONZALES, Erica. The music economy: the music services sector. 2016. Available at: <https://economiadeservicos.com/2016/09/06/a-economia-da- musica-o-sector-de-servicos-musicais/>. Accessed on: 16 Apr. 2018.

K19 TREINAMENTOS (Org.) Web Development with HTML, CSS and Javascript. 2013. Available at: <https://profsalu.files.wordpress.com/2014/11/k19-k02- desenvolvimento-web-com-html-css-e-javascript.pdf>. Accessed on: 21 Nov. 2017.

KLEINA, Nilton. The history of the Internet: pre-1960s to the 1980s: pre-1960s to the 1980s. 2011. Available at: <https://www.tecmundo.com.br/infografico/9847-a-historia-da-internet-pre-decada- de-60-ate-anos-80-infografico-.htm>. Accessed on: 13 Nov. 2017.

KOBYLINSKI, Diego. The influence of music on society. 2011. Available at: <https://inverta.org/jornal/edicao-impressa/445/cultura/a-influencia-da-musica-na- society>. Accessed on: 16 Apr. 2018.

KOTLER, Philip; KARTAJAYA, Hermawan; SETIAWAN, Iwan. Marketing 4.0: From Traditional to Digital. Rio de Janeiro: Sextante, 2017. 208 p.

LOPES, Daniel Francisco Ferreira et al. DEVELOPMENT OF AN ELECTRONIC PATIENT RECORD SYSTEM INTEGRATING HEALTH SERVICES. 2017. 26 f. TCC (Graduation) - Information Technology Management Course, Fatec Tatuí, Tatuí, 2017.

LOPES, Felipe Mariani; KOMURA, Gustavo Toshi. Website Building Course - HTML/CSS. 2011. Available at : <http://www.inf.ufpr.br/instrutores/arquivos/sites/html.pdf> Accessed on: 21 Nov. 2017.

LOPRETE, Bruno; LOPRETE, Fabricio. DIGITAL MARKETING. 2009. 13 f. Dissertation (Master's) - Unknown Course, Unknown, Lins-sp, 2009. Available at: <http://www.unisalesiano.edu.br/encontro2009/trabalho/aceitos/CC31 868805808.pdf>. Accessed on: 20 September 2017.

MARTINS, Daniela. Digital Marketing: Creating an uncomplicated e-book for volunteer groups. 2010. 173 f. Dissertation (Master's) - Multimedia Course, University of Porto, Porto, 2010. Available at: <https://repositorio- aberto.up.pt/bitstream/10216/59978/1/000143905.pdf>. Accessed on: 10 Nov. 2017.

MEYER, Maximilian. How did the Internet come about? 2014. Available at: <https://www.oficinadanet.com.br/post/13707-como-surgiu-a-internet>. Accessed on: 13 Nov. 2017.

NIEDERAUER, Juliano. Developing Websites with PHP. 2. ed. São Paulo: Novatec, 2011. Available at : <http://www.martinsfontespaulista.com.br/anexos/produtos/capitulos/650595.pdf>. Accessed on: 13 Nov. 2017.

NIEDERAUER, Juliano. Integrating PHP 5 with MySQL. São Paulo. Novatec Editora Ltda, 2005.

NUNES, Dimalice. Dropouts and informality hold down the country's unemployment rate: Delay in resuming economic growth continues to undermine formal employment and the persistence of those looking for vacancies. 2017. Available at: <https://www.cartacapital.com.br/economia/desistencia-e-informalidade-seguram-a- unemployment-rate-in-the-country>. Accessed on: 25 May 2018.

OBYLINSKI, Diego. The influence of music on society. 2011. Available at: <https://inverta.org/jornal/edicao-impressa/445/cultura/a-influencia-da-musica-na- society>. Accessed on: 16 Apr. 2018.

PAIVA, Jose Eduardo Ribeiro de. A critical analysis of the music/technology relationship from the post-war period to the present day. 1992. 106 f. Dissertation (Master's) - Arts Course, State University of Campinas, Campinas, 1992. Available at: <http://repositorio.unicamp.br/bitstream/REPOSIP/284336/1/Paiva_JoseEduardoRib eirode_M.pdf>. Accessed on: 16 Apr. 2018.

PALISCA, Claude V. HISTORY OF WESTERN MUSIC. 1st edition: November 1994 Gradiva. 1988.

PEREIRA, Ana Paula. What is CSS? 2009. Available at: <https://www.tecmundo.com.br/programacao/2705-o-que-e-css-.htm>. Accessed on: 08 Dec. 2017.

PIMENTA, Renan, Livro O Papel das Bandas de Música no contexto Social, Educacional e Artístico. 2010. Available at: <https://catalogobandasdemusicape.wordpress.com/origem-das-bandas/>. Accessed on: 13 Nov. 2017.

SANTOS, Felipe André dos. Marketing in the Digital Age: Analysing the Chico Rei brand. 2014. 59 f. TCC (Graduation) - Journalism Course, Federal University of Juiz de Fora, Juiz de Fora, 2014. Available at: <http://www.ufjf.br/facom/files/2014/03/Marketing-na-Era-Digital.pdf>. Accessed on: 11 Nov. 2017.

SANTOS, Marco Antonio Carvalho dos. The Importance of IT in Organisations. 2009. Available at: <https://www.baguete.com.br/artigos/636/marco-antonio- carvalho-dos-santos/29/05/2009/a-importancia-da-ti-nas-organizacoes>. Accessed on: 28 May 2018.

SANTOS, Roberta et al. Phonographic Market in the Digital Age: Changes and Trends from the Perspective of Experimental Telejournalism. 2016. Available at:

<http://portalintercom.org.br/anais/nacional2016/expocom/EX53-0298-1 .pdf>. Accessed on: 23 May 2018.

SEBRAE, Brazilian Micro and Small Business Support Service - MUSIC PLAYING BUSINESS: A GUIDE TO HELP YOU ENTREPRISE IN MUSIC. 2015. Available at: <http://www.sebraemercados.com.br/wp-content/uploads/2015/12/Musica_tocando_seu_negocio.pdf>. Accessed on: 16 Apr. 2018.

SEBRAE, Brazilian Micro and Small Business Support Service - MUSIC PLAYING BUSINESS: A GUIDE TO HELP YOU ENTREPRISE IN MUSIC. 2015. Available at: <http://www.sebraemercados.com.br/wp-content/uploads/2015/12/Musica_tocando_seu_negocio.pdf>. Accessed on: 16 Apr. 2018.

SILVA, Pricila Souza. Internet marketing. 2009. Available at: <https://ojs.eniac.com.br/index.php/Anais/article/view/10/13>. Accessed on: 11 Nov. 2017.

STECCA, Fabiana Letícia Pereira Alves; ÁVILA, Lucas Veiga. Marketing Management. Santa Maria: Colegio Politecnico, 2015. 86 p. Available at: <http://estudio01 .proj.ufsm.br/cadernos_cooperativismo/terceira_etapa/arte_gestao_marketing.pdf>. Accessed on: 27 May 2018.

STRALIOTTO, Ariadna. Why does communication need to be aligned with IT? 2016. Available at: <https://blog.operand.com.br/por-que-a-comunicacao-precisa- estar-alinhada-com-a-ti/>. Accessed on: 28 May 2018.

TEIXEIRA, Fabricio. What is Responsive Web Design? 2011. Available at: <https://brasil.uxdesign.cc/o-que-é-responsive-web-design-ab292eb616b7> Accessed on: 21 Nov. 2017.

ULYSSEA, Gabriel. INFORMALITY IN THE BRAZILIAN LABOUR MARKET: A REVIEW OF THE LITERATURE. 2005. Available at: <http://repositorio.ipea.gov.br/bitstream/11058/1926/1/TD_1070.pdf>. Accessed on: 25 May 2018.

Printed by Books on Demand GmbH, Norderstedt / Germany